Bitter Honey, Sweet Stings

Lune Kelly

BookLeaf
Publishing

India | USA | UK

Presentation by *BookLeaf Publishing*

Web: www.bookleafpub.com

E-mail: info@bookleafpub.com

ISBN: 9789360942342

First edition 2024

The stars in my sky have kept me afloat upon many a stormy sea. Thank you for shining on me as I found calmer waters.

into a river

       the clay of a mountain
              made from stones and blood
her ghosts too   of course

    facing the moon like a mirror
        could clay ever be to tall?

clay sits and is silent and -   the sea is
not still
               and I am

clay realizes life on her mountain
        scars and the sky on her shoulders
      could clay ever be so strong?

clouds above teach me the taste of rain
          I love the flavor of
knowing

          when sky clears she faces
me
clay faces the moon back and smiles
         I am still and so I
         cannot face the
         mountain in turn

she calls me a name that feels like an old
costume
            my skin crawls on hollow bones

                                    I have those?
                        skin and hollow -

    rock with the wind
          rock with the wind
       rock with the

    the moon is   the sky is making
    her thin
                                    the sea is not quiet
        and tide is out
           and clouds above teach me
                            the taste of rain

        the earth shifts underfoot
    what to do what to do

    follow the pull of the moon
                        downhill
                    to the

                    am I losing myself in

        no, I don't think so

the sea is not still
                     and I'm

follow the pull of the moon
                     the sea is deep and cold

am cold too
          and I think

               the sea is deep and dark and then

follow the pull of the moon
                     (the sea is dark and growing)
                     (warmer now)
                     (can it do that?)
                     (hammerheads circle like)
                     (vultures once did)

/my distance is quiet. does it hurt her?\

yes   I know
                                              I'm sorry
for what
                                        I like the sea
                                        I like the
                                   deep and dark
                                   cold and now the
                                 searing heat

I think I'm growing smaller and bigger
skin stretches over
bones creaking
shifting
like an old house
like coming home anew

don't see the moon for a while

my shoulders are soft
will not be a mountain and I

think I can live with that and I
miss the moon and the rain
the rain!

carries me to the sky with
dust and   stars meet me in
warm sunset

did the rain know my sorrow?
meet the dusk with a prisma of color before

the sky
drops me fast
dropping faster
before

awake twisted on dark earth and see

the stars!
     the moon!
my skin has never fit so well
        on my bones as full as bellies
    the mountain

     I twist and turn at will

I face her and
      am startled

     I stand at nearly her height

without lines

when I was tiny
    I understood that
        for things to be
            they must be made
                but when I saw the wrinkles
                    where my fingers bend
inward
"ah, bite marks!"
                "stop biting them, then"
I hadn't been
                    but that's what she'd said
              bite marks was just
            how I seemed to see
        the underside of my knuckles
noticed there was
            no border between
                the rest of the world
                        and me
                  and figured
whoever I was drawn by
            must have had a style
              without lines

gin and juice

peeling at an orange-round
        and put the sticker on your forehead
   you hand me two slices
           when I asked for one
a burst of sunset citrus
       tangerine warmth upon tongue
often poems escape poets
      in your absence I place
         the sticker on a forehead my own
and understand all the ones
       that make connections between
              sharing oranges
and

heartbeats

cat at the dog park

miniscule paws and
  whiskers baby-grass soft
   into a world so much bigger
than mine
   as far as the eye can see
  large creatures that don't
 look like me
voices booming and quick
   like thunder
    well-intentioned but when
   I try to play
  they flinch away
 do they think my swipes mean harm?
I don't mean to alarm but
   this murmer-chirp is all the voice I have
   and they don't know
    what I'm saying either
   tails thrashing fast
  must have said
something wrong again
  am I the only
  dog at this park
that doesn't quite bark
   and has whiskers?

chirp-and-motor

ask you a question
      answer with a bow of your head
           happily plant a kiss between
your ears
      your brow bears the initial of my truest
name
what name would you call me in your
              chirp-n-motor song
older than me when we met
      despite my bigger age
   your first step into my home
a blessing beyond words
        you fill the air in it's place with
    chirp-n-motor song
the light of it casts
     bone-shaped shadows
       on the innards of my skin
your cloud-warm presence to sharp contrast
          ivory daggers
      tear twine towers into memory
     and my beloved dried plants
   I'll pick more for you
a royal garden
      leaf and doomed-petal delicate

                    and later in the
night
                    a slice of salmon
              cook yours separate
          before I poison my portion with garlic
ask me a question with your chirp-n-motor song
              your brow bears the initial of my
truest name
          I place a kiss between your ears as an
answer

red wine and static

a new years night
      your room dark and in stasis
        I lay in it alone
            'nother plane of existence
                don't even
remember
                      where
you were
in my hand
      a solo-cup red of scarlet sadness
and on the screen
      a vhs tape I could only hope
          happened to be
             more haunted
                than me
dark square of a space
      of mind, of place
         girl with hair-inky comes
            through
the tv
   suggests a popsicle
        might make
          my glass of misery
            less
bitter

engine from my chest
                    sits on my stomach like stone
                            focus on her
rumble

                    hope it humbles
               the stagnant ache of
          red wine and static

dog and calm water

"you know I'm loyal as a dog to you"
desperate

pleading hands grip the beasts

talons

hungry

desperate?

monstrous

dragon daggers hold his belly
Grasp
Pull
Yank at her wrists

heave himself toward her until
Alas
it's belly meets his and his

bleeds

bleeds

into foamy ocean below him

                a circle of sharp stone and teeth
                        promise a death, quick and
painless

he falls he stares at the sea he

                        wonders if
                Icarus

                had a

                        view

                        like

        "at least a dog cannot lie
                                to the hand it bites"

what greets him is a storm
                jagged-stone cyclone
                                washing-machine
cycle
                sanguine viscera between
                        teeth

malicious

     desperate

monstrous

"but for a dog so trained
     you gnaw and whine
        like a
stray"

     he emerges from the sea
    on legs, tired
   from swimming
     he doesn't feel the scars
now

  did Icarus meet
    calm water

kettle song

I hold him to my lips and
     give him fire
  the smoke alarm blinks his spying red eye but
    holds his
       hollering tongue still
 is it medicine or poison?
I breathe him in and
  my throat gives us
    a sound like the steam of hot tea
it sings it's little kettle song

I hold him to my lips and give him
    a push
     just a suggestion
  definitely medicine
    my throat is kissed with cool lips
   the sound is softer now   breathe
in
 it sings it's kettle song
breathe out

                slowly, good
I hold him to my lips and he
   meets the back of my throat like ice
  the kettle song is quiet now

but is he any better?
we both know he's
worse
oh   but you love him so

like any vice

of course
I step outside
the sky is red
the peeping red eye blinks
his hollering tongue is
still?
my tongue turns to clay in my throat it
it sings it's kettle song   hurts
does it hurt?
I reach for
him?   the medicine but he is
not here
he is empty

The sky is red
I reach but he is
empty now

it's getting harder to breathe
it sings it's kettle song

the sky is red

why is his tongue   so still

It sings it's kettle song   it's

getting harder

to
breathe

the Empress

I lay one winter in my boots
    and follow the voice of a
stranger
   to find the face of a spirit that guides
  scented smoke lifts me from my body
settle in a meadow
   I've seen but never touched
    the wooden house isn't there
anymore
    because I've yet to build it
   meadow lined by forest
 my boots find in it a path
and at the end
  a river I've seen before
    so I know to my right is the
waterfall
    my boots make their way left
   sunlight kisses shoulders warm
  until the water is too inviting
 I swim until the river forks
split by a white stone that when laid up on
   warms me dry and my boots find
    a wooden staircase
    step down and it creaks
   and past it, more forest path

it leads me to an arch of white wicker
dripping with draping flower
            pass under and find
                    squares of garden beds
            so plump and lush with life
            surely wilt was nothing to them but
        distant fantasy
        fluffy-grass paths between them take me to
a gazebo, wicker-white and towering
            sit on it's rocking bench
                    wait as if expecting company
            a black cat
            bounds up
        presses itself to my thigh
    and darts away
            "that's not it" I think before
                    remembering what I meant by
    it

                    wait as if expecting company
            a red fox
            darts behind me to my left
            "not that either"
                    and before I know it
            at the other end of the bench
        A woman sits draped in black
            the sight of her like the eyes of a fawn
            that have seen my death
            and laughed

with the joys of my life
beforehand
the voice that guides, forgotten
urges I ask for a name
and I know I needn't
she doesn't speak
neither do I
how to describe
sitting the length of a swinging bench
from a body so clearly
celestial
I look down at my lap
a white-tailed doe
with ashen fur
rests her head on my thigh
I lift a hand to pet her
don't remember when I had to leave
I lay one winter in
my boots

cosmic dawn

found her in the fragment of a story
bathed in blood
and lavender
sword in hand
meets my gaze
never leaves her battles defeated
knew at once she was a part of me
her advice to me is heeded
and so my path stays straight
goblet gold and
crown on the ground
she rides a swan of lilac
always instructs me
follow my art
and my heart
even and especially when
it beats my ribs with fear
no guidance I'd sooner hear
than she who covers me
in sheets of green
and looks to me with
the colors of clouded sunrise

morning coffee

early-day clatter
        chitter-chatter of squirrels and birds
           young daylight drips through
window
         mug left to go cold on it's sill
      I've cracked it open for you
     spring-sweet of the air on
   your nose wet like dawn's dew
coffee-dark fur against
       coffee-cream-cool skin
         you chirp back to their
clamor
       of course that space in my chest
     is so comfortable to you
    it's where we've made your bed
   breeze on my naked back
  cheshire grin and engine-thunder-rumble
know I could weather any weather with you in it

the Emperor

I sit on the floor of my bedroom
cards and candle at my knees
wait and expect company
a man in black sits on my bed
and waits my turn before speaking
I ask how he'd like to be
painted
if he wishes I paint him at all
and there's a stall
before he answers
as he chooses words like bead-pearls
his metallic owl mask is still
a crown of blunt chrome on his brow
"I do not mind being depicted by you"
tells me
"Your art is a gift"
sitting quiet, someone shifts
not men of many words are we
don't exactly see his
hands but
know exactly how to hold mine
as I pin him under-brush
there's silence between when we speak
and when he leaves
it's before I know it

by then the wick's burned free
art and candle at my knees
I know he'll visit me again
in night-quiet

the Storm

lightening cracks
        a cold slap
                across my face
                ground crumbles underfeet
        against my will, forced to leave
    my chirp-n-motor heart behind me
her gaping absence
                bleeds past my knees
        I plead
    but it falls
on ears, unhearing or cruel
                        I mewl
                a kitten under
            uncaring current
        endless turrent of
    tack-stab-daggers in the wind
                    and wonder
                writhing
            why
    no one thought to warn me
when they saw
the kettle-pot-black of the sky

kits in clusters

clove of clustered flowers
                fireflies in trees
dragonfly with a message
                impulse with a key
one dark night
            my tongue slips
            wish to swallow it
            but you follow it
            and laugh
        save me from myself in the moment
is this how it feels in a confessional
        to be half
            of a puzzle
                with more than two pieces
            a drink too strong
                another night not long
                    enough for endless
conversation
            purr and kitten-quilt
        curl with you and wilt
        though inappropriate, when you do
    I'm sure even a certain doll
                could be envy-green
                        at the sweet
cat-nose-pink of you

haunted doll

somewhere muffled

snow and sleet

something distant

a fog, sickly-sweet

if it had any flavor at all

stand poised and tall

a doll, possessed puppet porcelain

movement not my own

how long had I been

walking, talking, while
asleep

body left on
autopilot

trying to pretend

to be me

slumber in snow and sleet

sit in a chair

a space in-between

and suddenly

my hands!
the backs of them!
in dizzying hd
run to bathroom mirror
in the

glass!

who is that I

see?

that's you
but isn't that
something you know

yes, but

if so

how come the wide of my

eyes

and the curve of my lips

are such news to me?

in the blood

victorious in their howling
        we hunted you
            chewed you
                buried your bones
       presumptuous wolves
         don't my ancestors know?
the blood on my hands
        the blood of path-sands
ahead and behind
       in body and mind
         it's in my root-stems too
my ancestors, their martyrs and survivors do
           we're seeds we're seeds we're
seeds !

but why would wolves know?
         when you bury seeds
            they grow

shadow drips in

paint my room in grayscale
winter and
moonless night
snowy stags bound o'er
plains of snowy sleet
doorway a sliver
of starless dark
at it's feet
a pitch paw!
sets timidly on icy floor
like doe into meadow
more of my guest drips o'er
bedroom moon-pale tile
blazing eyes, warm and wile
both locked onto
me!
careful steps into
a leap!
soot-dark joins me on my bed
doe into meadow
sets timidly o'er
snowy stag and sleet-silver
looks at me again
eyes aflame and
wide as sky drips back into

sliver-starless dark
      I wish the shadows goodnight

teddy and a rose

groves of trees that tower
stars scattered on the sea
dragonfly with a message
mushroom with a key
long hard shift at work one night
headlight kisses a tree
apologies galore with
nothing to to be sorry for
thought of you
having been
in the car alone
I would rather have sustained an injury
but how could I
sitting beside divinity
bright with life
shining sun
you're evergreen
at the store I see
teddy bear with rose-petal belly
and think of you

pillars three

I follow a child into battle
      she's protected by pillars three
         they track the case like
hounds
        though the crime never
mystery
       bring evidence from the dark
     I'm summoned by howls and barks
   a monster's remnant marks
she bears the same tattoo
    as me, and I chew on the thought
      that this girl, so small
       is the bravest being I've ever
seen
        like stone, heart and mind
are set
      I met this girl today and yet
     I'd kill for her last week
    as she sheds a tear at the stand
   mother pillar-hound readies to leap
    in an instant, if she does
      I'll stand between them and the
beast
     child soldier, courageous and
bee-sweet

      I showed up only to the final
confrontation
   do they know they're the ones who saved me?
I follow a child into battle
     she's protected by pillars three
        if she ever needs a fourth,
we know
              exactly where
I'll be

dragonflies and keys

thunder rumbles
towers crumble
as I tumble
into the sea
follow pull of the moon
and soon
land in hands
safe and warm
there's a swarm
of something poison-pretty
in my belly
knees like jelly
help find my footing
after so long on the ocean
there's a motion
in my chest
muscle sore from not using
tired from wounding
and neglect and yet
help stop my bleeding
find myself needing
a lifetime of
making you dinner
what a winner I

am

to know
you

ought to show you
all the best that I can be
grow vivid and strong
the journey is long
but with you, it'll be
evening-pretty stroll breeze
bring me ease
and ravens three
our paths cross-wind
and so we find along the way
dragonfly with a message
cards that guide to thee
a puzzle with more than
two pieces
you reflect on my surface like the moon
picture without you
incomplete
push and pulled by your tide
do we think I could be the
sea

ducks and hot coffee

sipping slowly, coffee hot
at night and plot
to bring chirp-n-motor heart to me
read tomes of law
and write my own
of reasons to keep her
from claws that scar my belly
hard to tell, he
acted with willing to hurt
but if it's her, see
could he consider an act of mercy
make my plead
to storm uncaring
thought a red herring
was all I
need but
knows I bleed without
her
brags about how
lonely she is without him
how he's always out and
thinks he can atone
for always leaving her alone
with a few feeble minutes of sunshine
his stories a field of landmines

of all the ways he gets her wrong
his travesty try at translating
her chirp-n-motor
song
she doesn't
belong
with a dog who won't meet her
needs
and keep her pleased
with a life cream-sweet
the way any cat deserves
know she hurts
from reading cats all my life
it fills me with strife how
he looks at her like one in a
million
when in my eyes
she's one of a kind and priceless
any price is
less than I'd be willing to pay
to spend the rest of
my days
making up for every moment of
her having been left
behind
set heart and mind
and know
my purring home
poised on her throne

is coming with me to stay
clear as day
I'm where she's meant to be
cavity in my chest
though never as empty
as her place next to me
there's something strong and beating
it's burning in her bed
sword ready in my hands
lining up my ducks
oh fate and luck my
heart of chirp-n-motor
when it's over
you'll never be left lonely again
for as long as you live to be
and I'll be sure to make it last
a cuddly-cat's
eternity

www.ingramcontent.com/pod-product-compliance
Lightning Source LLC
La Vergne TN
LVHW010826200726
843508LV00012B/2515